Don't Step On That Earwig

Don't Step On That Earwig

Compiled and illustrated by
Rowena Sommerville

RED FOX

A Red Fox Book

Published by Random House Children's Books
20 Vauxhall Bridge Road, London SW1V 2SA

A division of Random House UK Ltd
London Melbourne Sydney Auckland
Johannesburg and agencies throughout the world

First published in 1992 by Hutchinson Children's Books

Red Fox edition 1993

Text in this edition © Hutchinson Children's Books 1992
Illustrations © Rowena Sommerville 1992

This book is sold subject to the condition that it shall not, by way of trade or otherwise, be lent, resold, hired out, or otherwise circulated without the publisher's prior consent in any form of binding or cover other than that in which it is published and without a similar condition including this condition being imposed on the subsequent purchaser.

The right of Rowena Sommerville to be identified as the illustrator of this work has been asserted by her in accordance with the Copyright, Designs and Patents Act, 1988.

Designed by Rowan Seymour

Printed and bound in Great Britain by
Cox & Wyman Ltd, Reading, Berkshire

RANDOM HOUSE UK Limited Reg. No. 954009

ISBN 0 09 927441 8

For my parents

Contents

Hurt No Living Thing *Christina Rossetti* 9

Flitters
A Gnat *Helen Ratcliffe* 12
Bee *George Barker* 13
The Old Man of Tralee *Edward Lear* 14
The Fly *Walter de la Mare* 15
Julius Caesar and the Honey Bee *Charles Tennyson Turner* 16
Nature Study *Moira Andrew* 17
An Unconsidered Trifle *Helen Ratcliffe* 18
Sizewise *Rowena Sommerville* 20
The Butterfly *Anon* 21
The Butterfly and the Kite *Raymond Wilson* 22
Adventure *Louis Untermeyer* 23
Mottled Moths *Pamela Gillilan* 24
What Do You Suppose? *Anon* 25

Critters
Don't Step on That Earwig *Rowena Sommerville* 28
Spider *Gina Douthwaite* 32
Earwig O! *Eric Finney* 34
The Gone Locusts *George Awoonor-Williams* 35
Clock-a-clay *John Clare* 36
On the Grasshopper and the Cricket *John Keats* 37
Spider *Alan Brownjohn* 38

The Grasshopper and the Elephant *Anon*	40
The Centipede *Carmen Bernos de Gasztold*	41
Silverfish Rap *Rowena Sommerville*	42
Ants Although Admirable Are Awfully Aggravating *Walter R Brooks*	44
The Termite *Ogden Nash*	45
Incey Wincey's Lament *Rowena Sommerville*	46
Anancy! *Manley Young*	48
A Game of Squash *Dick King-Smith*	49
Look Said the Boy *Michael Rosen*	50
Close Encounter *Rowena Sommerville*	52
Cobweb Morning *June Crebbin*	54
Khepra *Rowena Sommerville*	57
The Stick Insect *Gavin Ewart*	58

Leapers and Creepers

The Lambton Worm *Traditional story*	60
Snails *Liagarang*	62
The Sick Rose *William Blake*	63
The Tickle Rhyme *Ian Serraillier*	64
Dissertation on the Antiquity of Fleas *Anon*	65
Crunch Thwock *Rowena Sommerville*	66
Worms and the Wind *Carl Sandburg*	68
The Song of the Flea *Johann von Goethe*	70
The Snail *William Cowper*	72
Today I Saw A Little Worm *Spike Milligan*	73
Surprise! *Helen Ratcliffe*	74
Acknowledgements	76

Hurt No Living Thing

Hurt no living thing;
Ladybird, nor butterfly,
Nor moth with dusty wing,
Nor cricket chirping cheerily,
Nor grasshopper so light of leap,
Nor dancing gnat, nor beetle fat,
Nor harmless worms that creep.

CHRISTINA ROSSETTI

Flitters

A Gnat

A gnat —
What's that?
— ouch —
Drat!!

HELEN RATCLIFFE

Bee

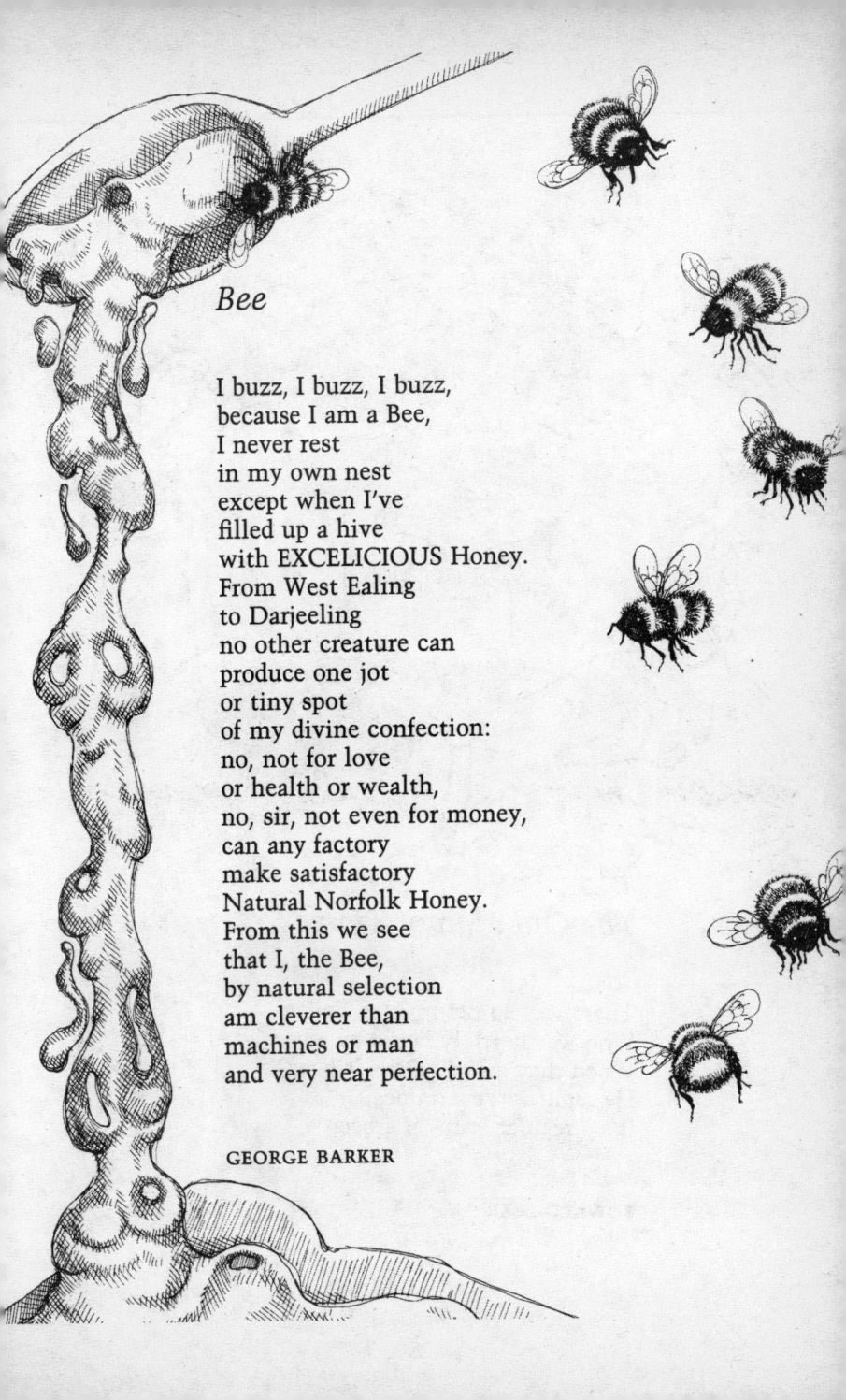

I buzz, I buzz, I buzz,
because I am a Bee,
I never rest
in my own nest
except when I've
filled up a hive
with EXCELICIOUS Honey.
From West Ealing
to Darjeeling
no other creature can
produce one jot
or tiny spot
of my divine confection:
no, not for love
or health or wealth,
no, sir, not even for money,
can any factory
make satisfactory
Natural Norfolk Honey.
From this we see
that I, the Bee,
by natural selection
am cleverer than
machines or man
and very near perfection.

GEORGE BARKER

The Old Man of Tralee

There was an old man of Tralee,
Who was horribly bored by a bee.
When they asked, 'Does it buzz?'
He replied, 'Yes, it does,
It's a regular brute of a bee.'

EDWARD LEAR

The Fly

How large unto the tiny fly
Must little things appear! –
A rosebud like a featherbed,
Its prickle like a spear;

A dew-drop like a looking glass,
A hair like golden wire;
The smallest grain of mustard-seed
As fierce as coals of fire;

A loaf of bread, a lofty hill;
A wasp, a cruel leopard;
And specks of salt as bright to see
As lambkins to a shepherd.

WALTER DE LA MARE

Julius Caesar and the Honey Bee

Poring on Caesar's death with earnest eye,
I heard a fretful buzzing on the pane:
'Poor bee!' I cried, 'I'll help thee by-and-by;'
Then dropped mine eye upon the page again.
Alas, I did not rise; I helped him not:
In the great voice of Roman History
I lost the pleading of the window bee,
And all his woes and troubles were forgot.
In pity for the mighty chief who bled
Beside his rival's statue, I delayed
To serve the little insect's present need;
And so he died for lack of human aid.
I could not change the Roman's destiny;
I might have set the honey-maker free.

CHARLES TENNYSON TURNER

Nature Study

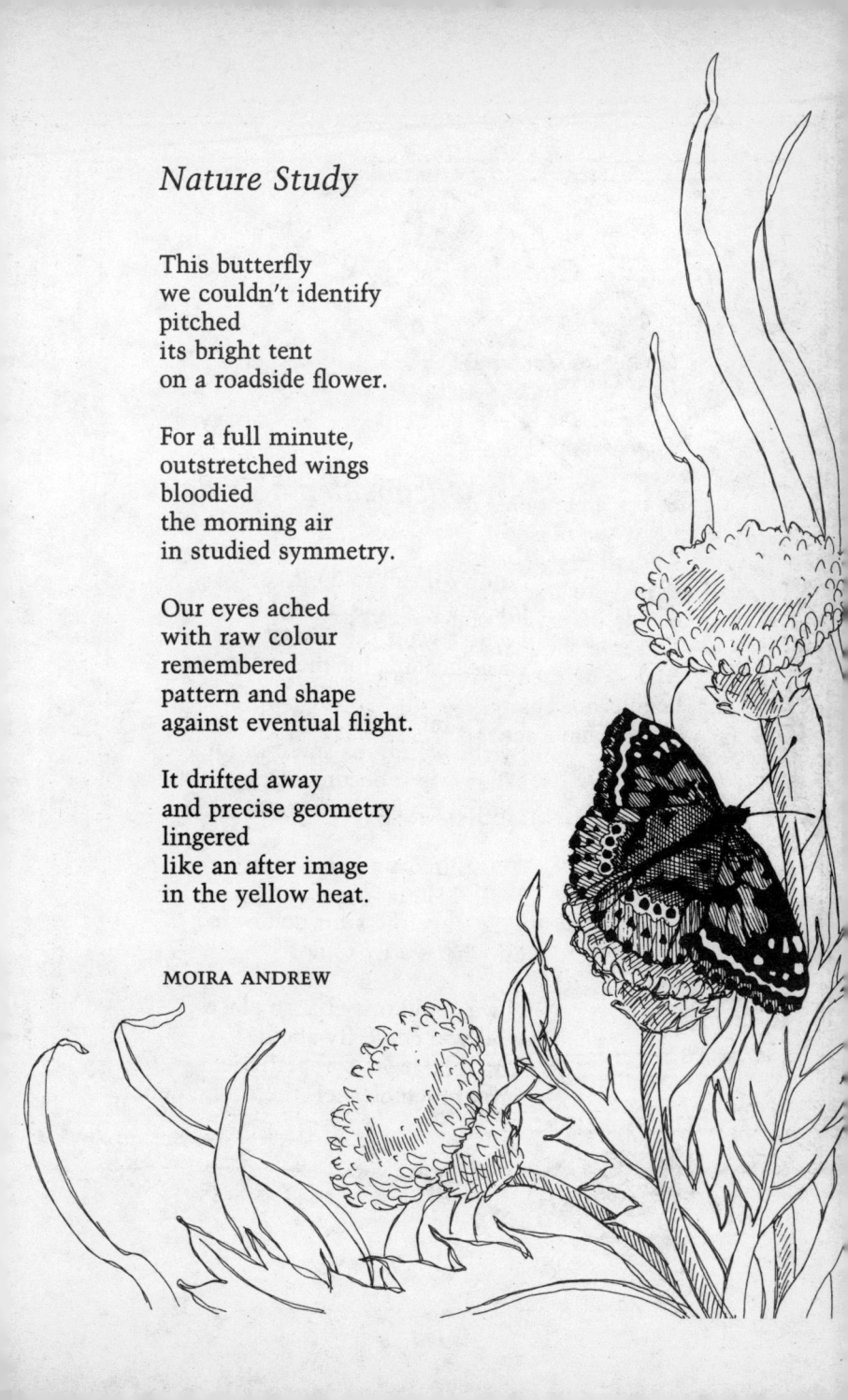

This butterfly
we couldn't identify
pitched
its bright tent
on a roadside flower.

For a full minute,
outstretched wings
bloodied
the morning air
in studied symmetry.

Our eyes ached
with raw colour
remembered
pattern and shape
against eventual flight.

It drifted away
and precise geometry
lingered
like an after image
in the yellow heat.

MOIRA ANDREW

An Unconsidered Trifle

I didn't mean to do it,
It's not my fault at all,
I didn't want the trifle,
I was heading for the wall.

I got a bit distracted
By the wondrous smell of rot –
What was it decomposing
On the cooker in that pot?

You think my habits nasty,
Well, I think yours are too,
You leave the stuff uncovered,
So what's a fly to do?

If we could just change places,
And you could fly about,
You'd be more sympathetic
(And much cleaner) there's no doubt.

But – you're rolling up your paper,
You want to squash me flat,
You chase me round the windows –
I don't think much of that!

And now the grand finale
The spray is coming out,
'I'll get that pesky creature!'
I hear you scream and shout.

You've sprayed the room, you're checking,
And you think that I've been shooed,
But just be very careful
Of what's floating in your food!

HELEN RATCLIFFE

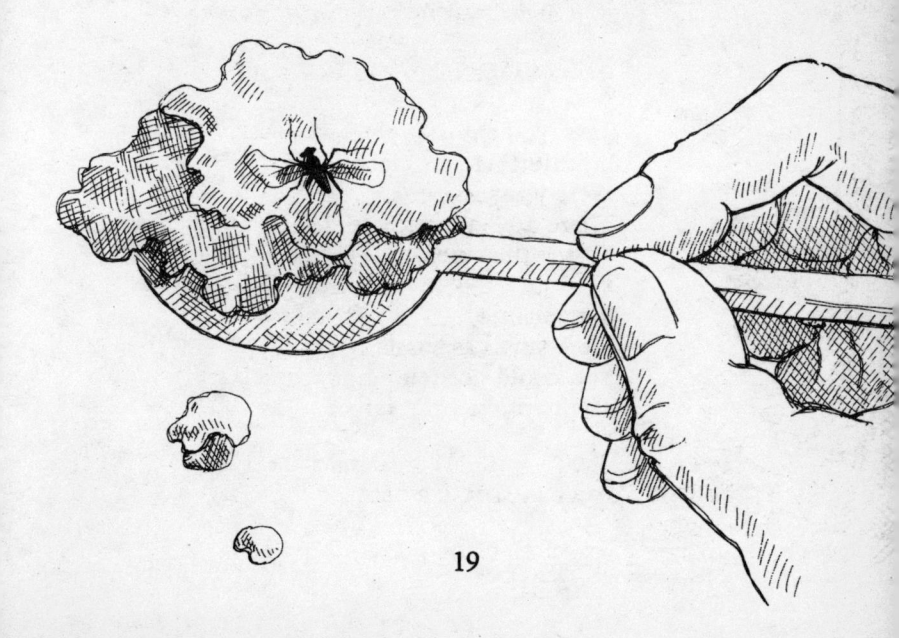

Sizewise

If butterflies
Were jumbo-size,
There'd be no space
To see the skies.

If elephants
Were small as snails,
You could not tell
Their trunks from tails.

ROWENA SOMMERVILLE

The Butterfly

I always think the butterfly
Looks best against the clear blue sky;
I do not think he looks so good
Pinned down within a box of wood.

ANON

The Butterfly and the Kite

Taller than hills or trees,
   A paper kite
Dancing upon the breeze
Looks down to earth and sees
Zig-zagging to and fro
   Far, far below,
A butterfly in flight.

Still soaring haughtily,
   The kite calls down:
'Take a good look at me!
How would you like to be
Dancing above the world,
   Wind-swept and swirled
Over country and town?'

'Not on your terms,' replied
   The butterfly.
'Puffed out with wind and pride,
Can you not see you're tied?
Who wants to be the toy
   Of a stupid boy? –
Better go free than go high!'

RAYMOND WILSON
adapted from a Russian fable by Krylov

Adventure

The moon said:
'I will show you gardens more lavish than the sun's;
Flowers more magical;
Stranger enchantments, heavier odours.
Come.'

And the butterfly followed
Down to a distant sea;
And perished
Trying to perch on the foaming blossoms
Of moonlit waves.

LOUIS UNTERMEYER

Mottled Moths

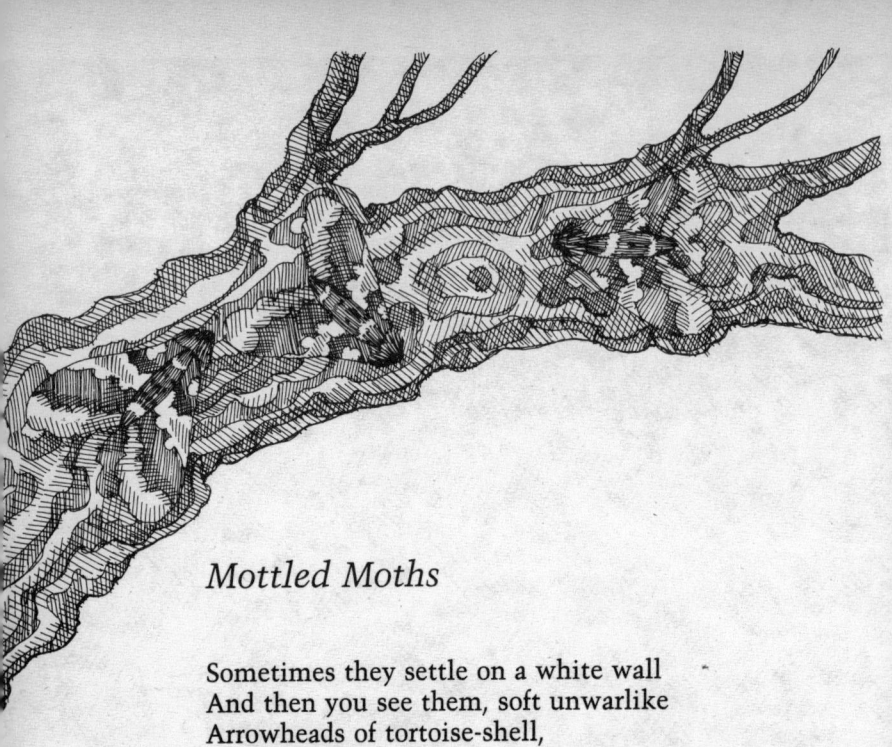

Sometimes they settle on a white wall
And then you see them, soft unwarlike
Arrowheads of tortoise-shell,
Cream and brown.

But they are tree bark
Or old stone, and can stay safe
And invisible all day
On the unsheltered rock,
The wild tree.

They sleep and bask hidden
By their own openness,
Though birds that are always hungry
Live on the same branch.

PAMELA GILLILAN

What Do You Suppose?

What do you suppose?
A bee sat on my nose.
Then what do you think?
He gave me a wink,
And said, 'I beg your pardon,
I thought you were the garden!'

ANON

Critters

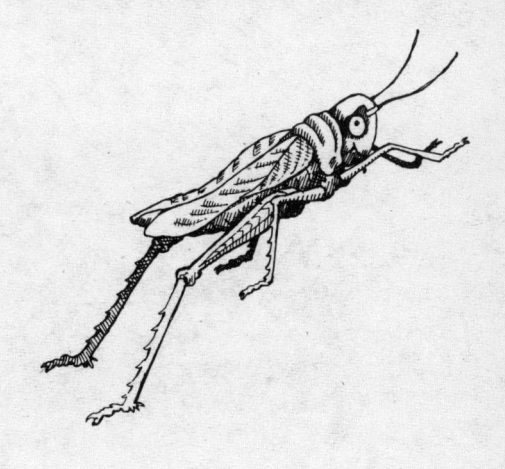

Don't Step on That Earwig

Careful, don't step on that earwig,
It's some earwig's baby for sure,
Do you want the soul of that earwig
On your conscience, your foot, or the floor?

Perhaps you think earwigs are ghastly?
Perhaps when you see one you run?
But they want the same things as you do,
Like friendship and freedom and fun.

And earwigs feel love and affection,
Their hearts can beat fast with delight,
They may hide in cracks in the daytime,
But they dance cheek to cheek through the night.

Now earwigs make excellent parents,
They care for their children, it's true,
They guard them and feed them and lick them,
Would yours do the same thing for you?

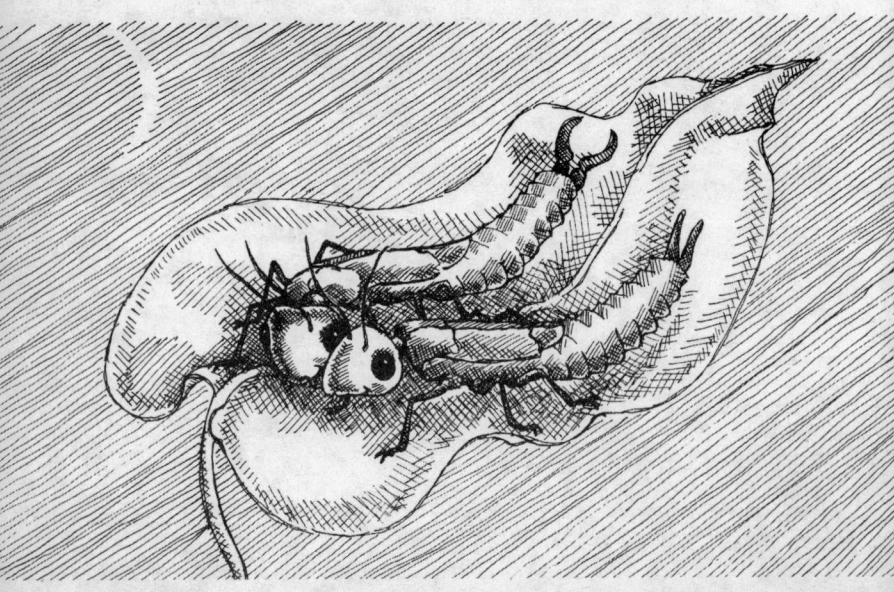

They teach all their children good manners,
And train them to run away fast,
And tell them a story at bedtime
From *Great Earwig Escapes of the Past*.

In summer they may go on outings,
And sometimes they go to the sea,
Where they potter and paddle and picnic
With prime earwig titbits for tea.

In winter they don't venture out much,
They stay safe and cosy indoors,
And ski down the legs of the tables,
And skate on the clean polished floors.

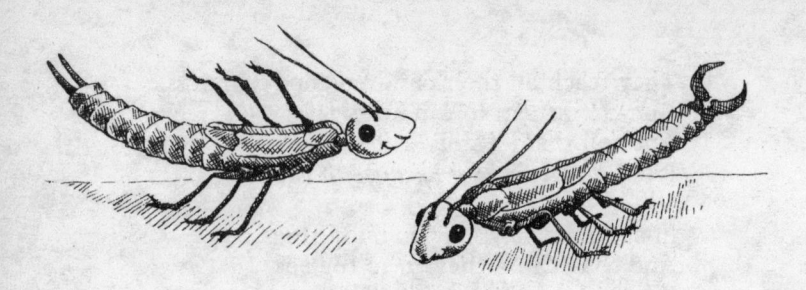

But all of the fun and the frolics
Can never make up for the pain,
When one little earwig gets careless
And parents are waiting in vain.

Oh, can you imagine the worry?
The world is a dangerous place,
Where everything's bigger than you are,
And strangers go 'UGH!' in your face.

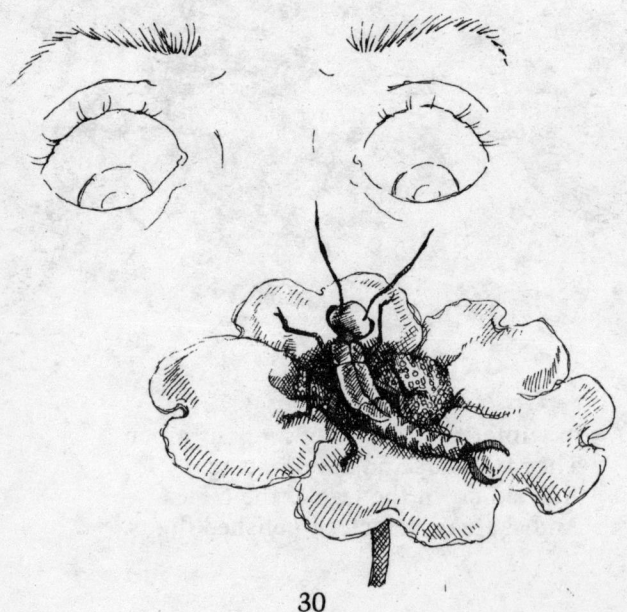

For the earwig's a victim of slander,
'They nip with their pincers,' it's said,
'And then they creep in through your nostrils,
And wander about in your head.'

But this is just absolute nonsense,
You can't believe all that you hear,
The earwig is loving and gentle –
What's that —
   crawling out of ——
                YOUR EAR?

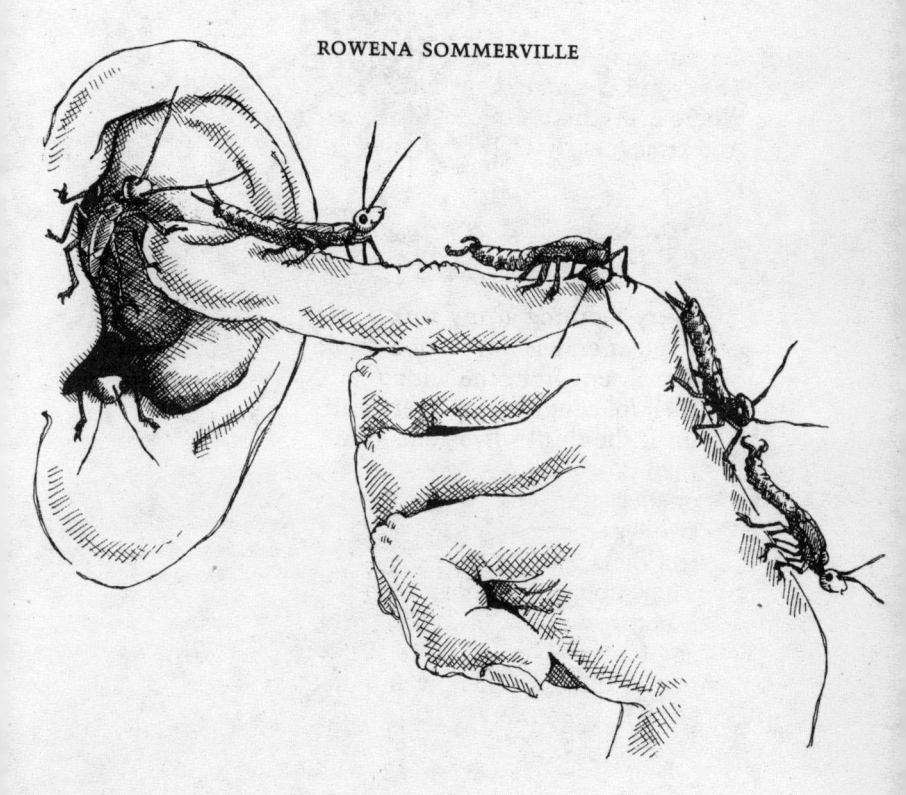

ROWENA SOMMERVILLE

Spider

Every morning at my sink
a spider crawls down for a drink.
She abseils from the windowsill
then folds up, keeping very still
until she thinks I've gone away
then
one leg
two legs,
feel their way.
They prod, they probe,
legs three
and four
join in the fun. Then even more!

Legs five
and six
extend and lift
hydraulically – she tilts a bit
till hairy members
seven
and eight
receive their message, 'ACTIVATE'.
And so, across the soapy trickle,
she flits! – black threads of silky tickle –
till tidal waves, tipped from the bowl,
send her whirlpooling down the hole . . .
then

one leg,
two legs,
feel their way . . .

GINA DOUTHWAITE

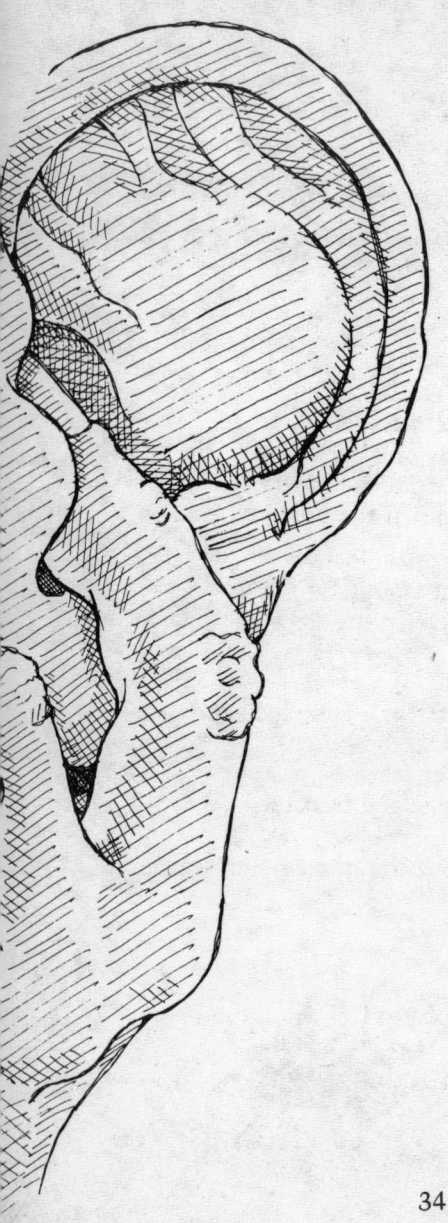

Earwig O!

They used to fear
That while asleep
Into the ear
This beast would creep;
Through waxy passages
Would tread
To penetrate
The very head,
Until at last
It would attain
The grey and wrinkled
Human brain
Where, after pausing
For the view,
It probably
Would start to chew . . .

Believe this,
You must be a dope.
It's just
An old wives' tale.

I hope . . .

ERIC FINNEY

The Gone Locusts

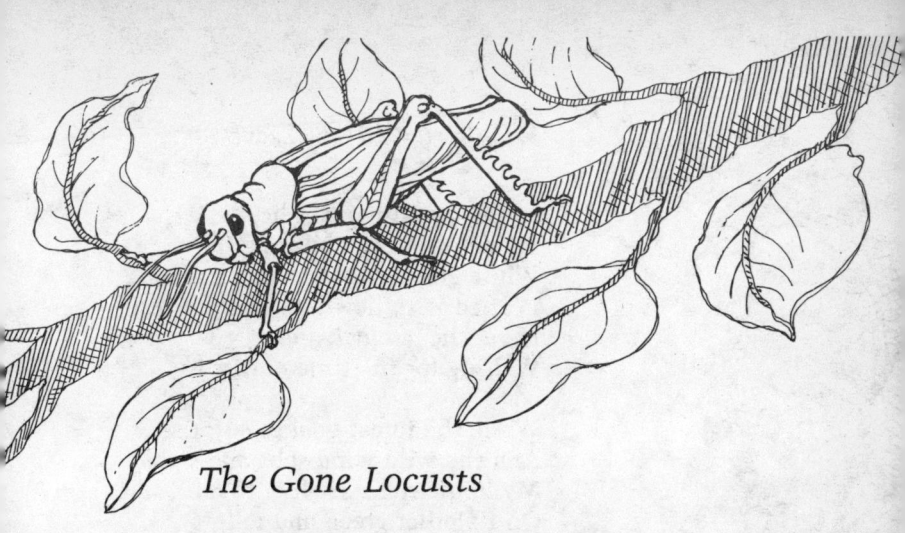

I saw treetops from the desert land
And wished I could pluck the green leaves
And make myself a hut.

I sat there and watched the locusts
From the east come in clouds,
And then the green tops of the trees
Were no more.

Then I and the trees and the gone locusts
Became the desert dwellers,
Yet I shall be under the trees
And the rains will come and beat me.

I shall wish for the return of the sowing season,
In which the farmer
Will forget his harvest.

GEORGE AWOONOR-WILLIAMS

Clock-a-clay (Ladybird)

In the cowslip pips I lie,
Hidden from the buzzing fly,
While green grass beneath me lies,
Pearled with dew like fishes' eyes,
Here I lie, a clock-a-clay,
Waiting for the time of day.

While the forest quakes surprise,
And the wild wind sobs and sighs,
My home ricks are like to fall,
On its pillar green and tall;
When the pattering rain drives by
Clock-a-clay keeps warm and dry.

Day by day and night by night,
All the week I hide from sight;
In the cowslip pips I lie,
In rain and dew still warm and dry;
Day and night, and night and day,
Red, black-spotted clock-a-clay.

My home shakes in wind and showers,
Pale green pillar topped with flowers,
Bending at the wild wind's breath,
Till I touch the grass beneath,
Here I live, lone clock-a-clay,
Watching for the time of day.

JOHN CLARE

On the Grasshopper and the Cricket

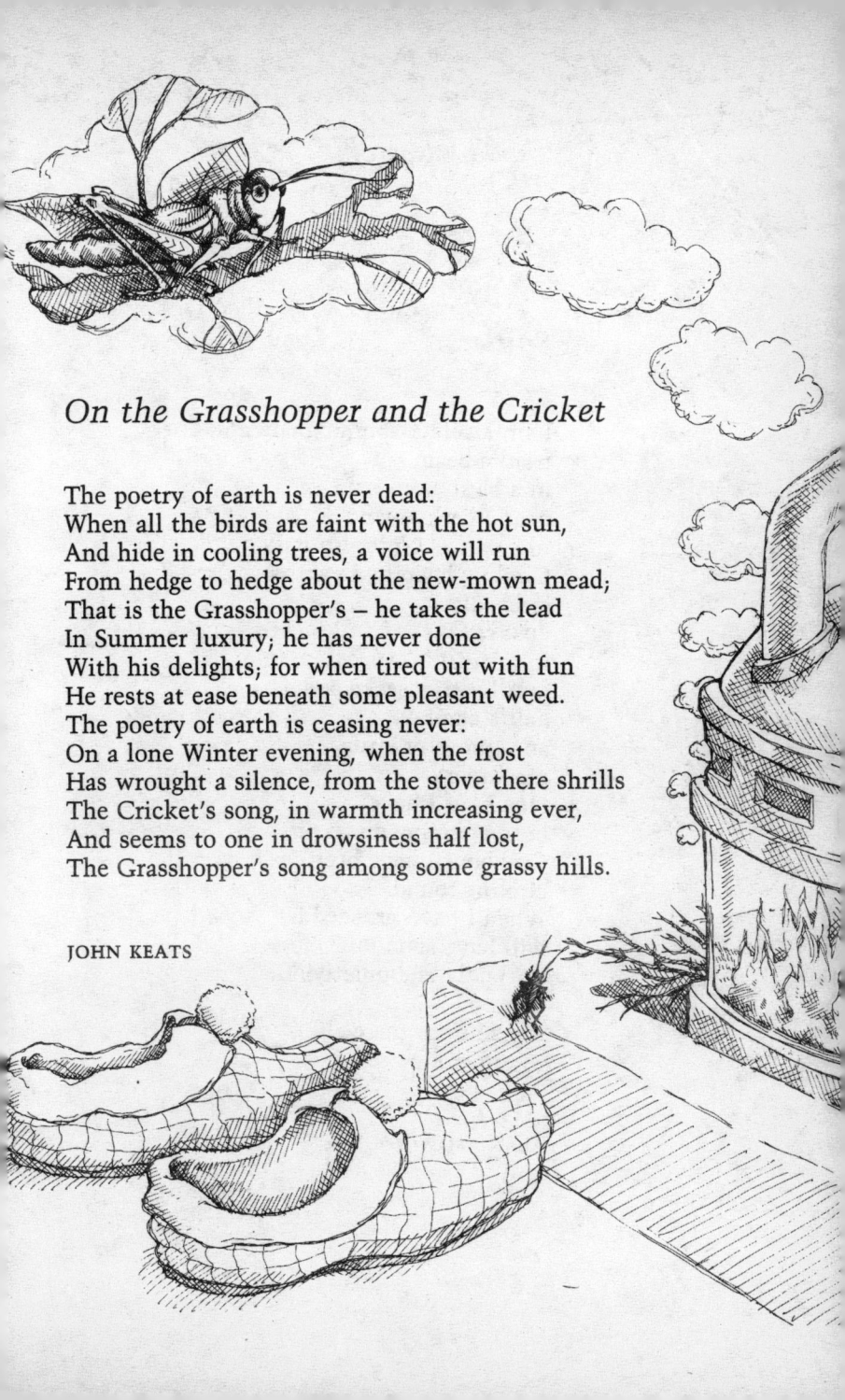

The poetry of earth is never dead:
When all the birds are faint with the hot sun,
And hide in cooling trees, a voice will run
From hedge to hedge about the new-mown mead;
That is the Grasshopper's – he takes the lead
In Summer luxury; he has never done
With his delights; for when tired out with fun
He rests at ease beneath some pleasant weed.
The poetry of earth is ceasing never:
On a lone Winter evening, when the frost
Has wrought a silence, from the stove there shrills
The Cricket's song, in warmth increasing ever,
And seems to one in drowsiness half lost,
The Grasshopper's song among some grassy hills.

JOHN KEATS

Spider

I am a spider spinning down
from a beam
in a barn
near a little town
in a part of Northern Italy.
Circling happily, I can see
(past idle
dust specks
in the air)
four hessian sacks and
half a chair
and lumps of farm
machinery.
One hour I have
been spinning down,
One hour I have been
circling round.
When I have finished I
will have spun
(invisibly and quietly)
One
thread from the ceiling
to the ground.

ALAN BROWNJOHN

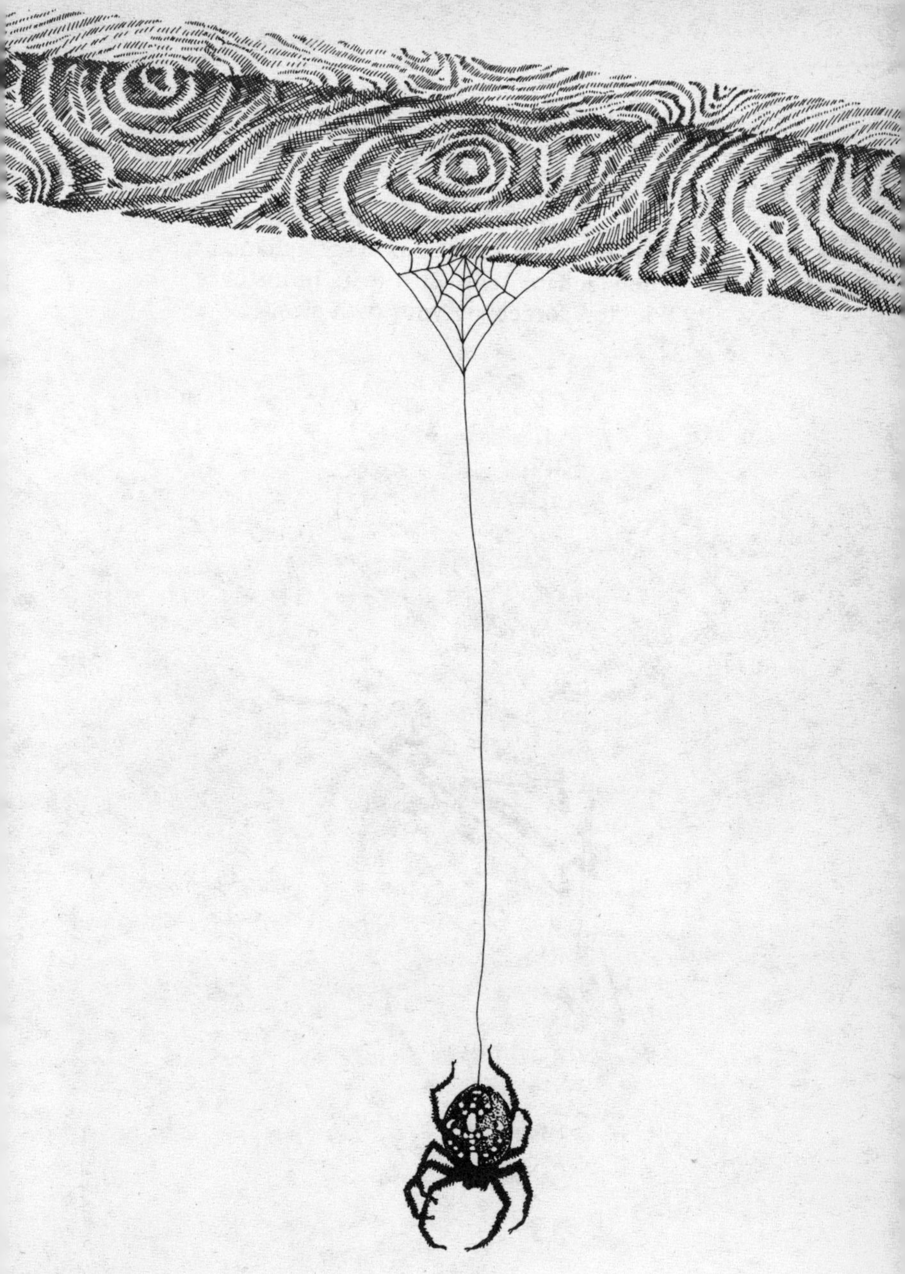

The Grasshopper and the Elephant

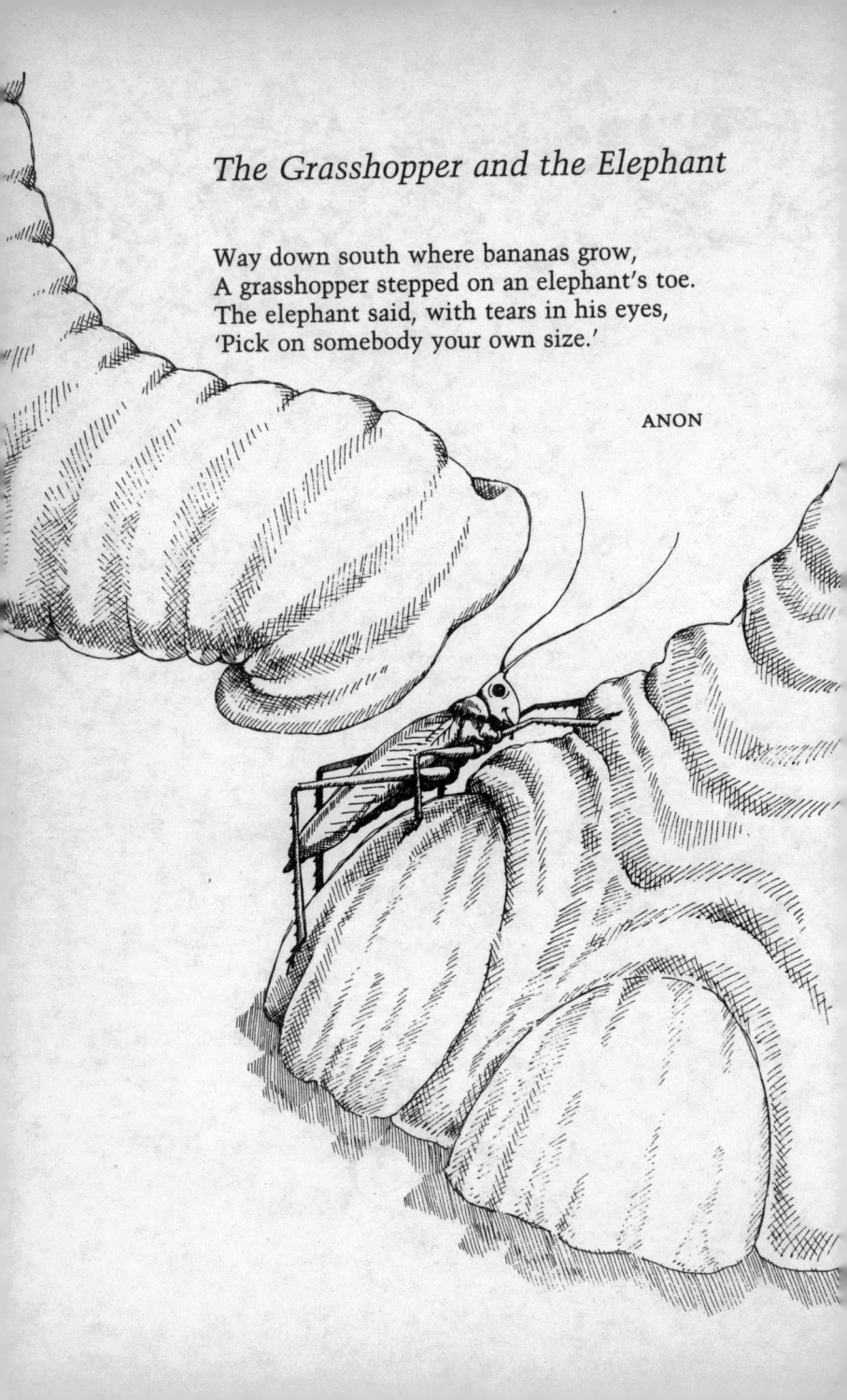

Way down south where bananas grow,
A grasshopper stepped on an elephant's toe.
The elephant said, with tears in his eyes,
'Pick on somebody your own size.'

ANON

The Centipede

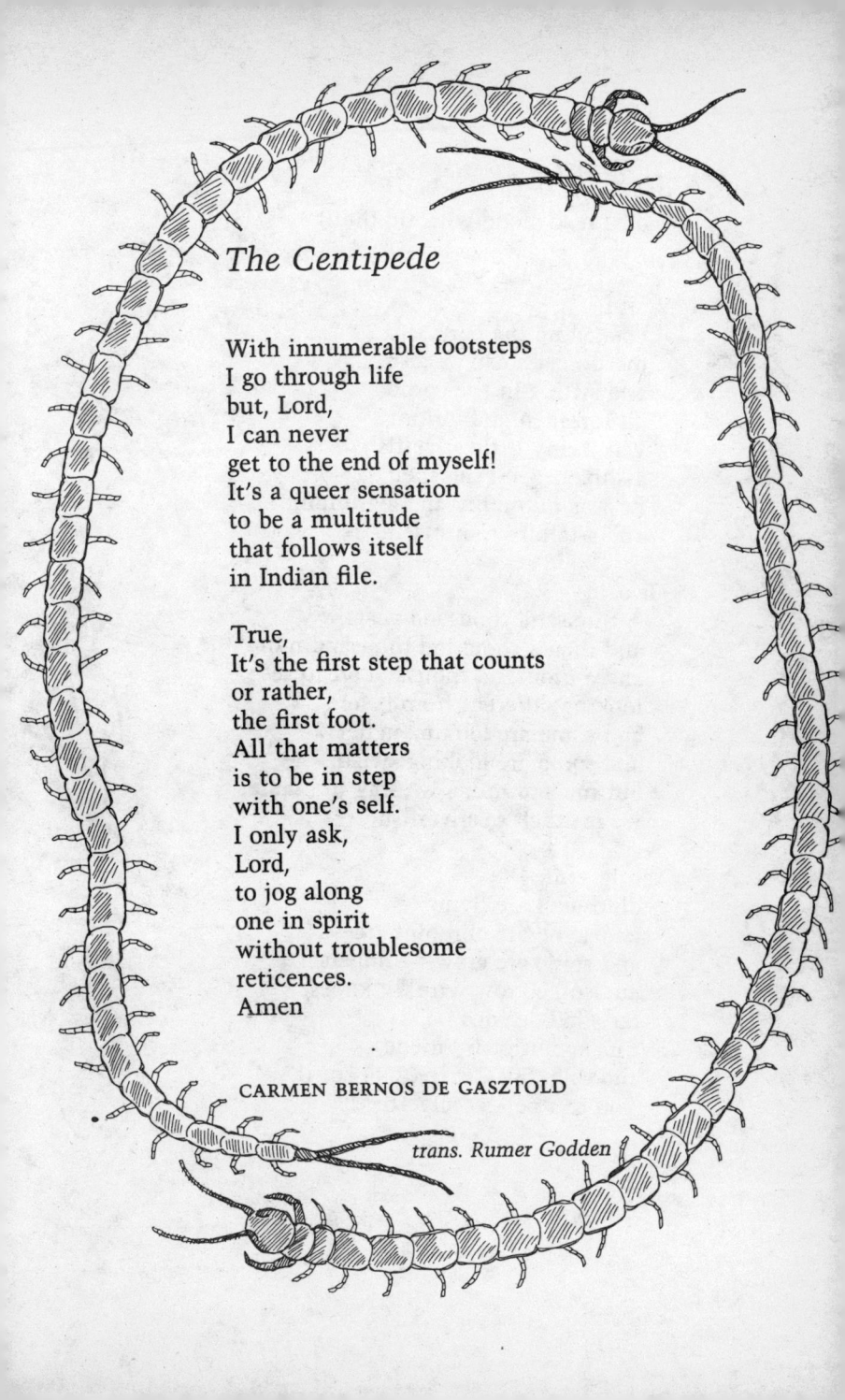

With innumerable footsteps
I go through life
but, Lord,
I can never
get to the end of myself!
It's a queer sensation
to be a multitude
that follows itself
in Indian file.

True,
It's the first step that counts
or rather,
the first foot.
All that matters
is to be in step
with one's self.
I only ask,
Lord,
to jog along
one in spirit
without troublesome
reticences.
Amen

CARMEN BERNOS DE GASZTOLD

trans. Rumer Godden

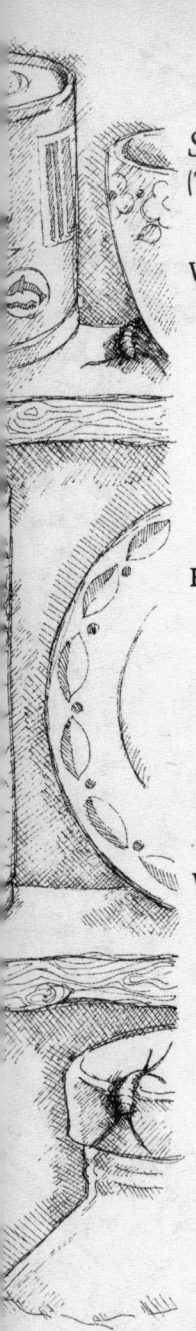

Silverfish Rap
(To be read aloud with rhythm!)

Well I
   opened up the cupboard
   just to get a can of corn,
   and sitting in the corner
   all forsaken and forlorn,
   was a tiny little silverfish
   a-shivering on the shelf,
   he was mumblin' and a-grumblin'
   and a-talkin' to himself.

He said –
   A thousand thousand years,
   and then a thousand thousand more,
   and a thousand thousand creatures
   looking different from before,
   and some are looking uglier
   and some are looking swish,
   but me and mine, we stay the same,
   we're stuck as silverfish.

While some
   dinosaurs are flying
   and some are climbing trees,
   and some are growing fingers
   and some grow wrinkly knees,
   but God decided on
   this evolutionary niche,
   and said, 'By George, I've got it!
   You're a perfect silverfish!'

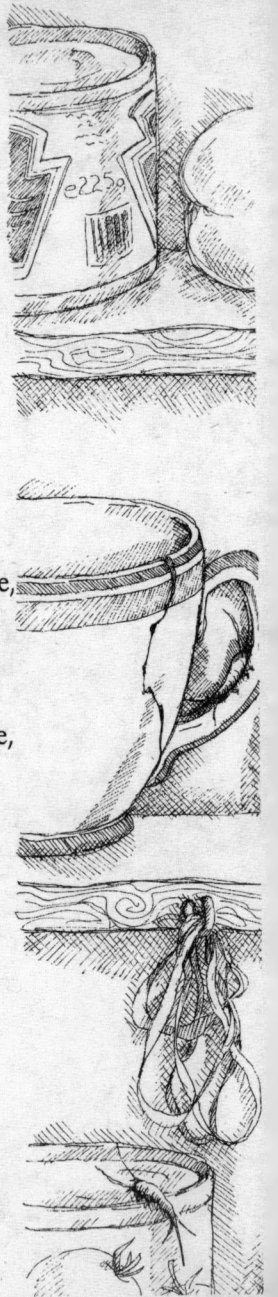

I don't
   like to keep complaining,
   but each day it's getting harder,
   and my world view is restricted
   to the inside of the larder,
   I'm not asking for a miracle,
   I don't want revolution,
   but I'd like a small development,
   I'd like some evolution.

And I'd
   like to climb a mountain
   and to see what 'sunrise' means,
   and I'd like to read some books,
   not just the labels on the beans,
   and I'd like to swim the ocean,
   and I'd like to play the drums,
   and I'd like a change from sitting
   in this cupboard, eating crumbs.

Well I
   closed the cupboard door
   and then I made a cup of tea,
   and I thought about this creature
   and its static history,
   and if I think my life is dull,
   and not just what I'd wish,
   I'll still be very grateful
   that I'm not a silverfish!

ROWENA SOMMERVILLE

Ants Although Admirable Are Awfully Aggravating

The busy ant works hard all day
And never stops to rest or play.
He carries things ten times his size,
And never grumbles, whines or cries.
And even climbing flower stalks,
He always runs, he never walks.
He loves his work, he never tires,
And never puffs, pants or perspires.

Yet though I praise his boundless vim
I am not really fond of him.

WALTER R. BROOKS

The Termite

Some primal termite knocked on wood,
And tasted it and found it good,
And that is why your Cousin May
Fell through the parlour floor today.

OGDEN NASH

Incey Wincey's Lament

Crowds of thoughtless children
Have learnt to sing and shout,
With the tale of Incey Wincey
And that never-changing spout.

Sunburst after sunburst,
Rainburst after rain,
There goes Incey Wincey,
Again, again, again.

I'd like children better
If one at mother's knee,
Should think of all that effort,
And how it feels for me.

Do they think there's nothing
for a spider in her prime
To do, but climb that drainpipe
For the thirty thousandth time?

I could go to parties,
I could dance at spider balls,
I could slip through plugholes
And leap out on bathroom walls.

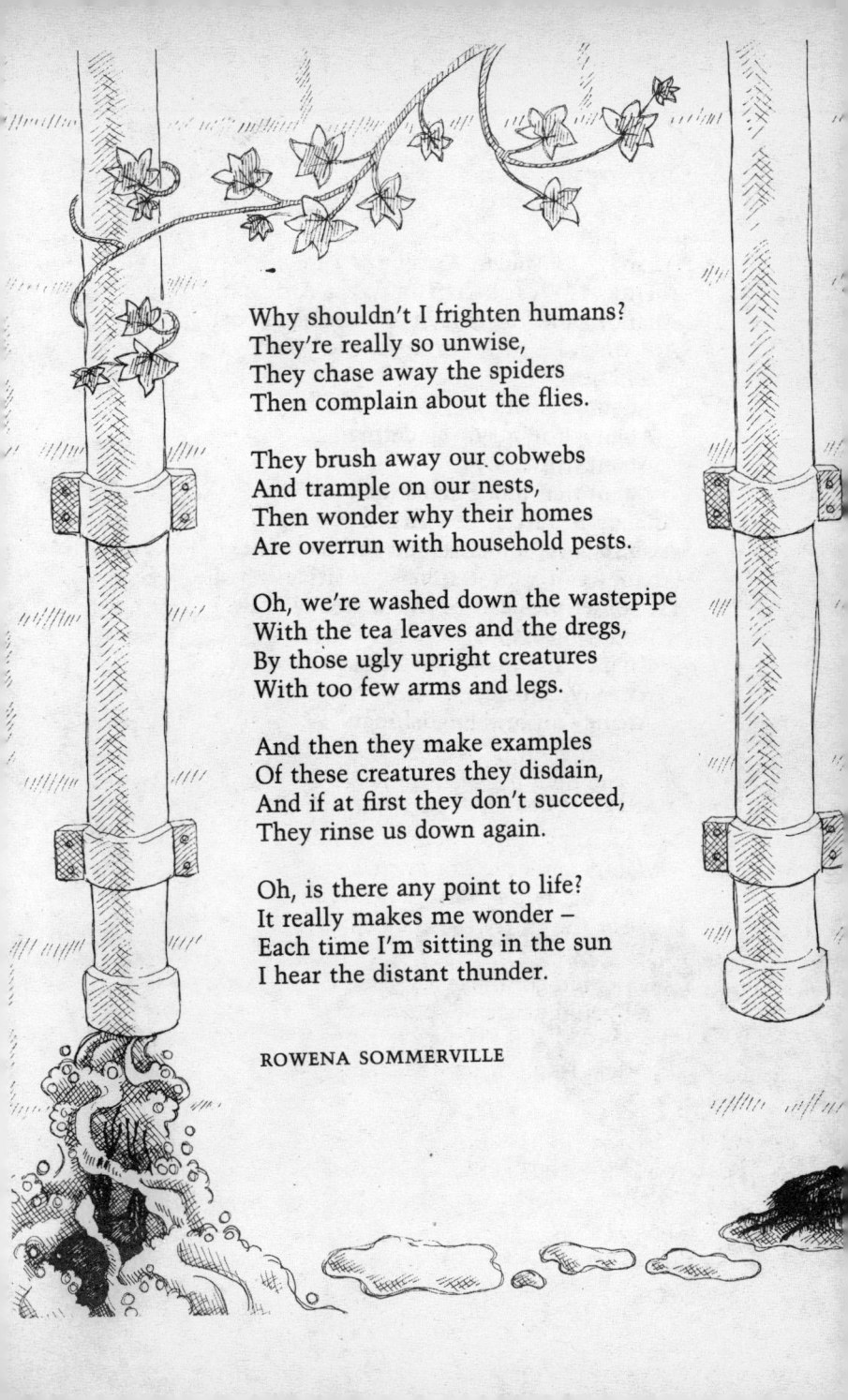

Why shouldn't I frighten humans?
They're really so unwise,
They chase away the spiders
Then complain about the flies.

They brush away our cobwebs
And trample on our nests,
Then wonder why their homes
Are overrun with household pests.

Oh, we're washed down the wastepipe
With the tea leaves and the dregs,
By those ugly upright creatures
With too few arms and legs.

And then they make examples
Of these creatures they disdain,
And if at first they don't succeed,
They rinse us down again.

Oh, is there any point to life?
It really makes me wonder –
Each time I'm sitting in the sun
I hear the distant thunder.

ROWENA SOMMERVILLE

Anancy!

Anancy is a spider, Anancy is a man,
Anancy is West Indian an' West African.
Anancy sailed to Englan' on a banana boat
An' when he got to Brixton, everybody gave
  A shout:
  Anancy, Anancy!
  Anancy the magic spiderman.
  Anancy, Anancy!
  Anancy an brer Englishman.
Anancy is a jiver, he's frisky as a fly,
A shifty plastic being, and that is no lie.
Anancy is a trickster, he's sensitive to guile,
He sometimes can be like a greedy chile.
  Anancy, Anancy!
  Anancy the magic spiderman.
  Anancy, Anancy!
  Anancy an brer Englishman.

MANLEY YOUNG

A Game of Squash

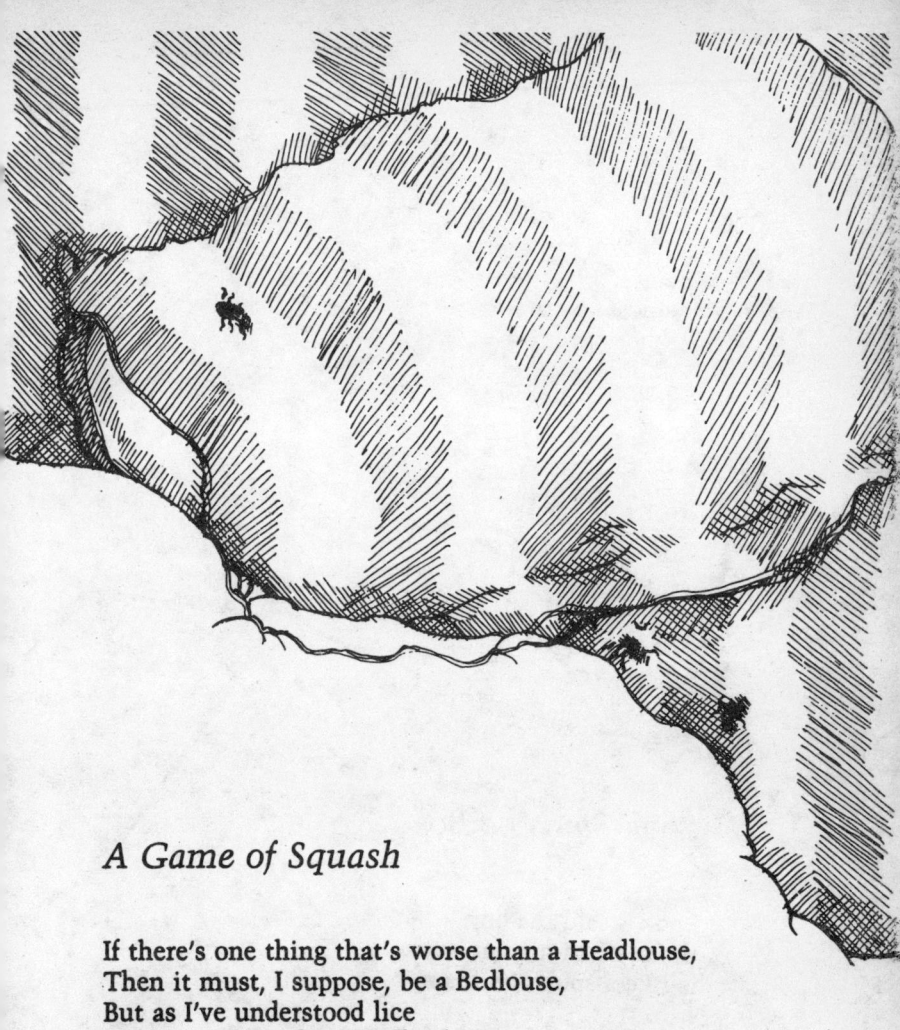

If there's one thing that's worse than a Headlouse,
Then it must, I suppose, be a Bedlouse,
But as I've understood lice
(And excepting the Woodlice),
Why, the only good louse is a dead louse.

DICK KING-SMITH

Look Said the Boy

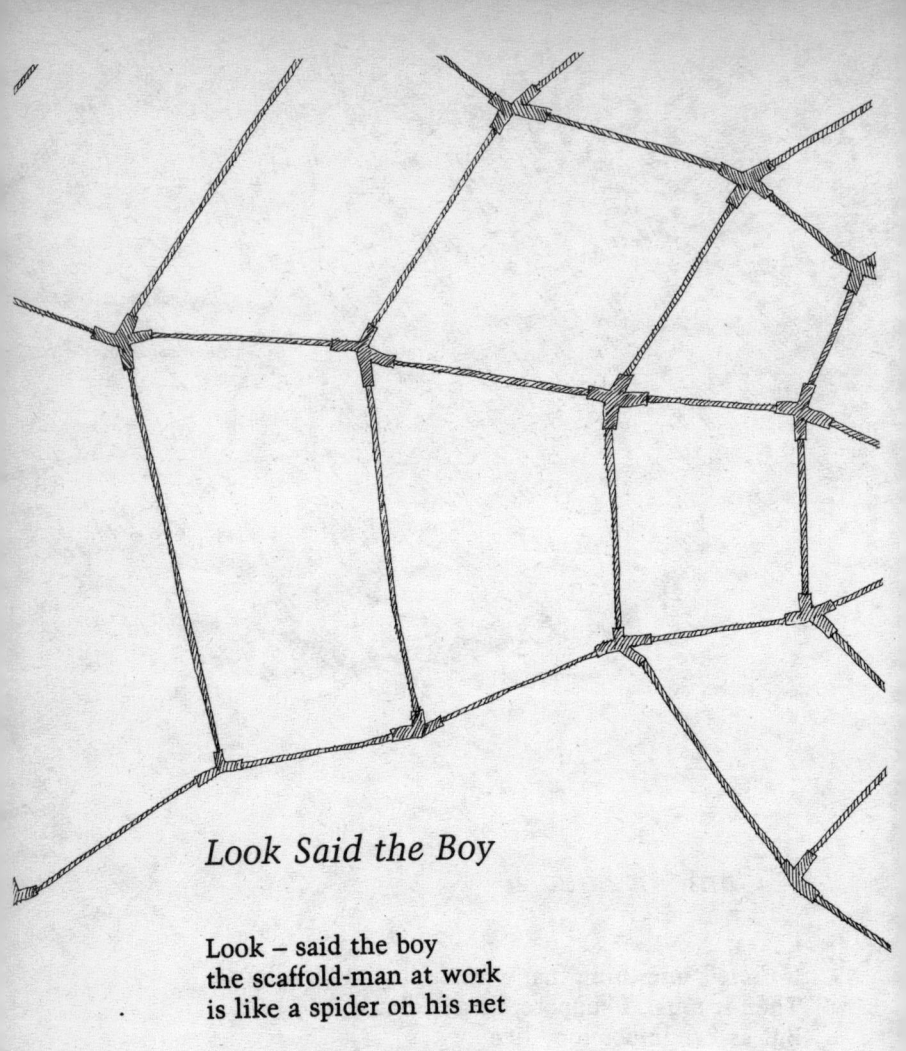

Look – said the boy
the scaffold-man at work
is like a spider on his net

No – said the scaffold-man
I'm just a fly
in the trap the spider set

MICHAEL ROSEN

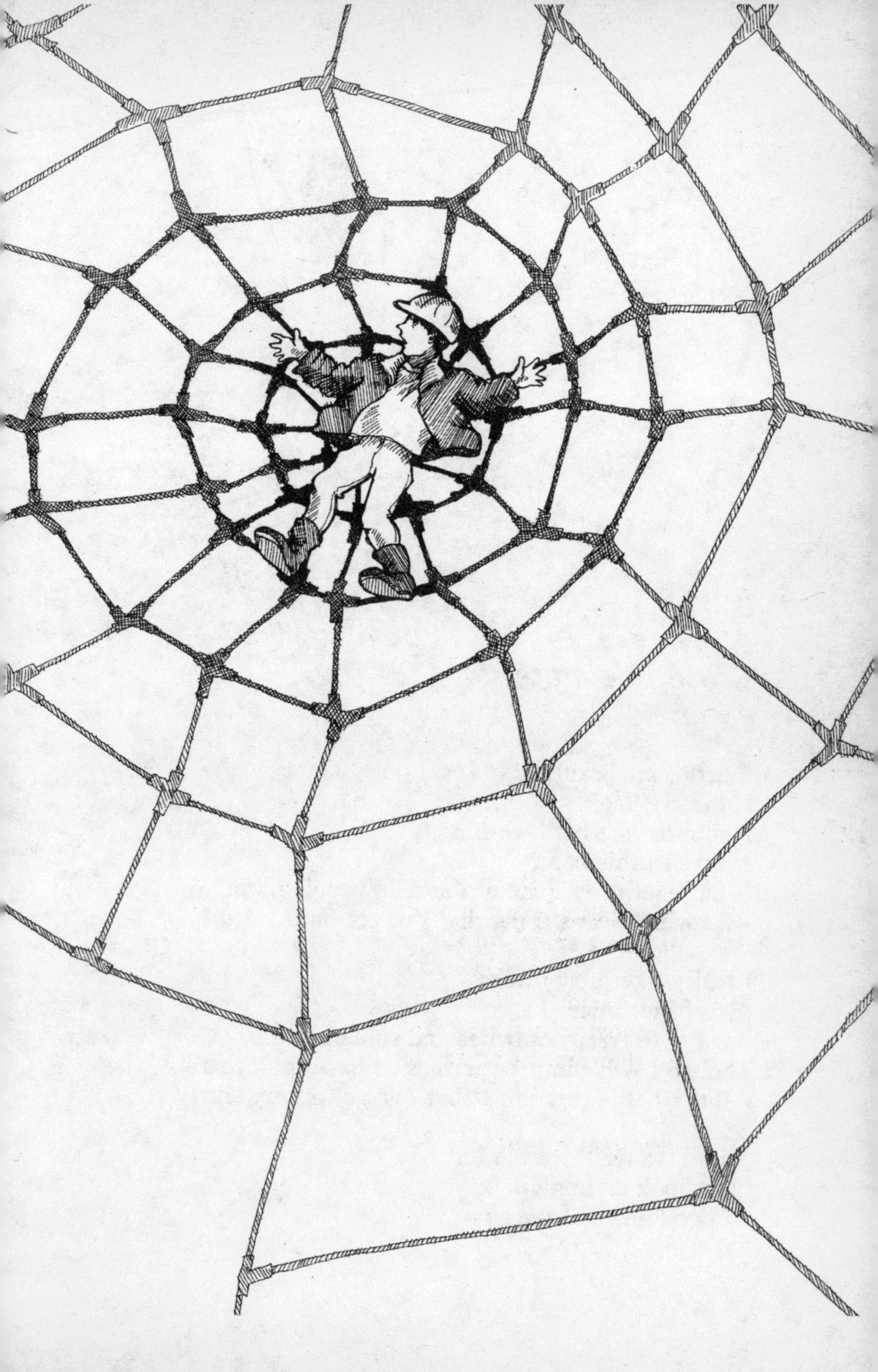

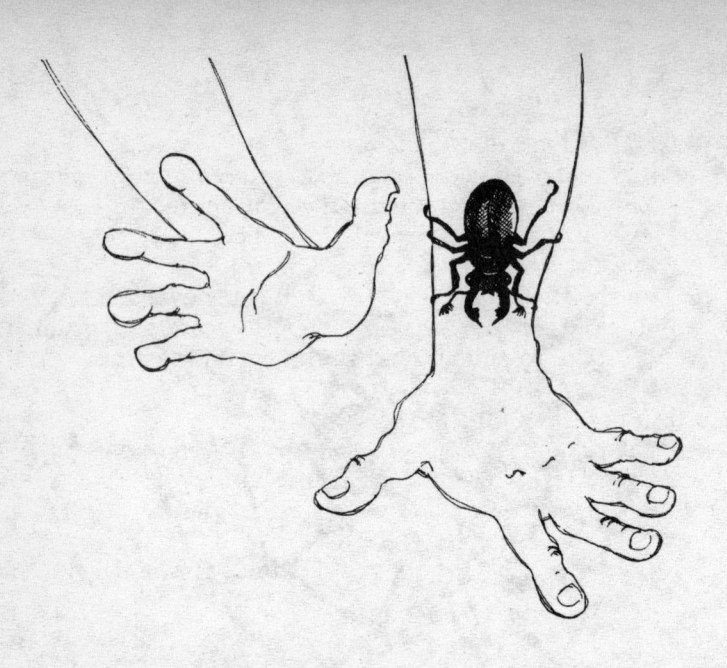

Close Encounter

'Beetles are beautiful,
Honestly, look,
And most are hard-working,'
It says in this book,
'And practically none of them do people harm,'
– So what is this thing that I've got on my arm?

I really like furry things,
(Except for mice),
But I hate creepy-crawlies and spiders and lice,
Though I will admit butterflies do have their charm,
– But what is this thing that I've got on my arm?

Miss says we'll learn a lot
('Just look around'),
So I've looked at the sky

And I've looked at the ground,
And I've looked in my book and I've tried to keep calm
– But what is this thing that I've got on my arm?

Miss says I'm lucky it's landed on me,
And she's called the whole class to come over and see,
But while they're all giggling, there's sweat on my palm,
All caused by this thing that I've got on my arm.

Miss says it's lovely
('The find of the day') –
Though just what it is, she's unable to say
And now even she's showing signs of alarm,
– SO WHAT IS THIS THING THAT I'VE GOT –
                                   Oh, it's flown away.

ROWENA SOMMERVILLE

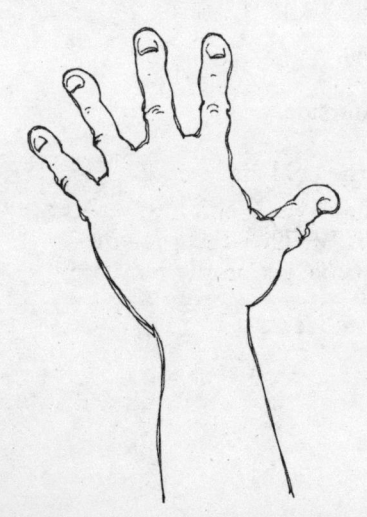

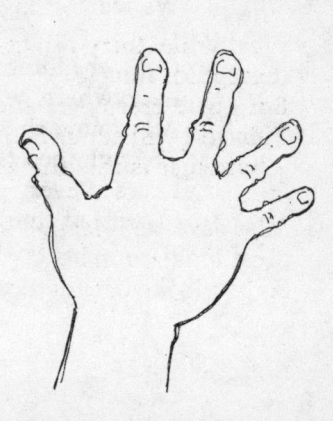

Cobweb Morning

On a Monday morning
We do spelling and maths
And silent reading.

But on the Monday
After the frost
We went straight outside.

Cobwebs hung in the cold air,
Everywhere.
All around the playground,
They clothed the trees,
Dressed every bush
In veils of fine white lace.

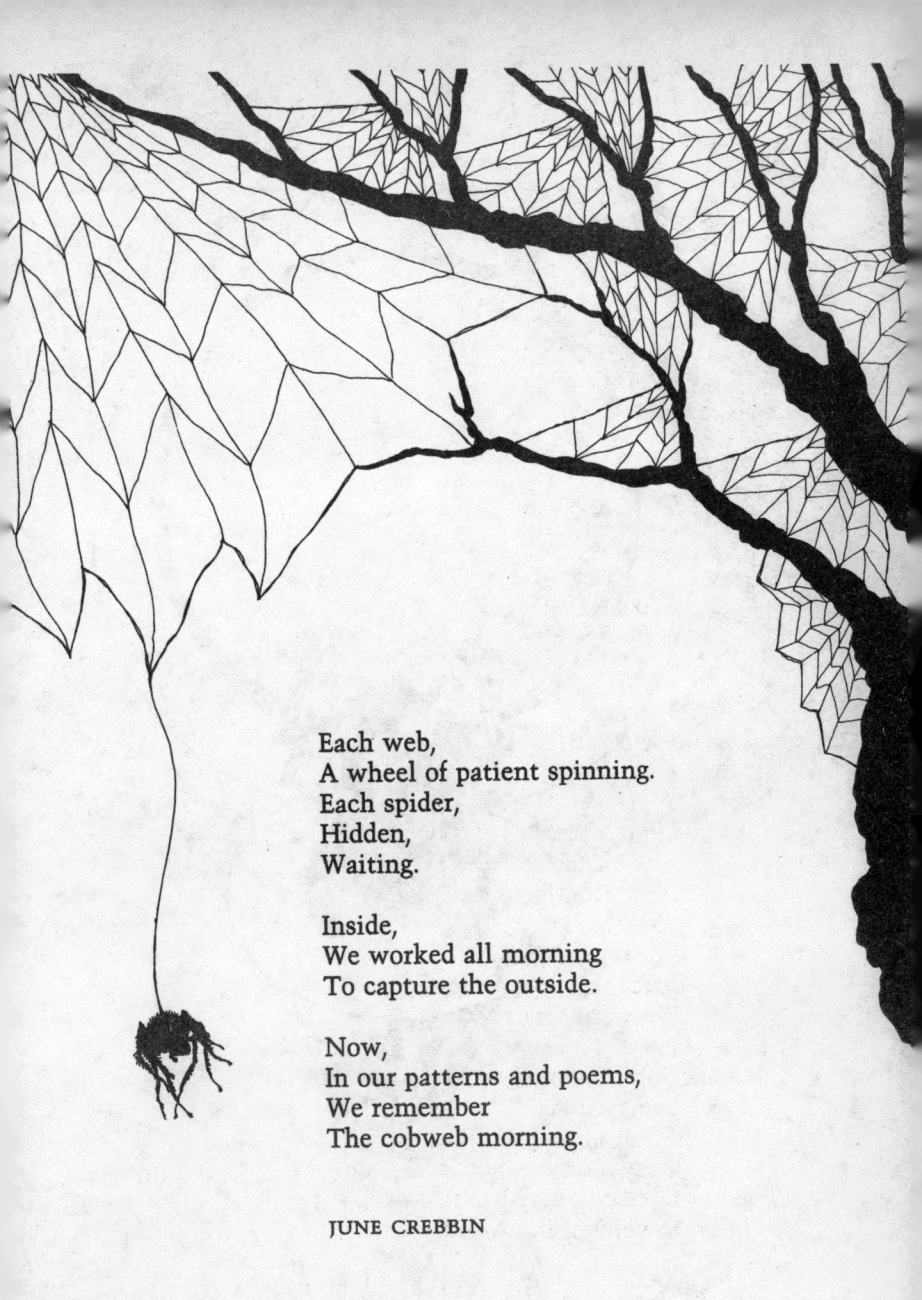

Each web,
A wheel of patient spinning.
Each spider,
Hidden,
Waiting.

Inside,
We worked all morning
To capture the outside.

Now,
In our patterns and poems,
We remember
The cobweb morning.

JUNE CREBBIN

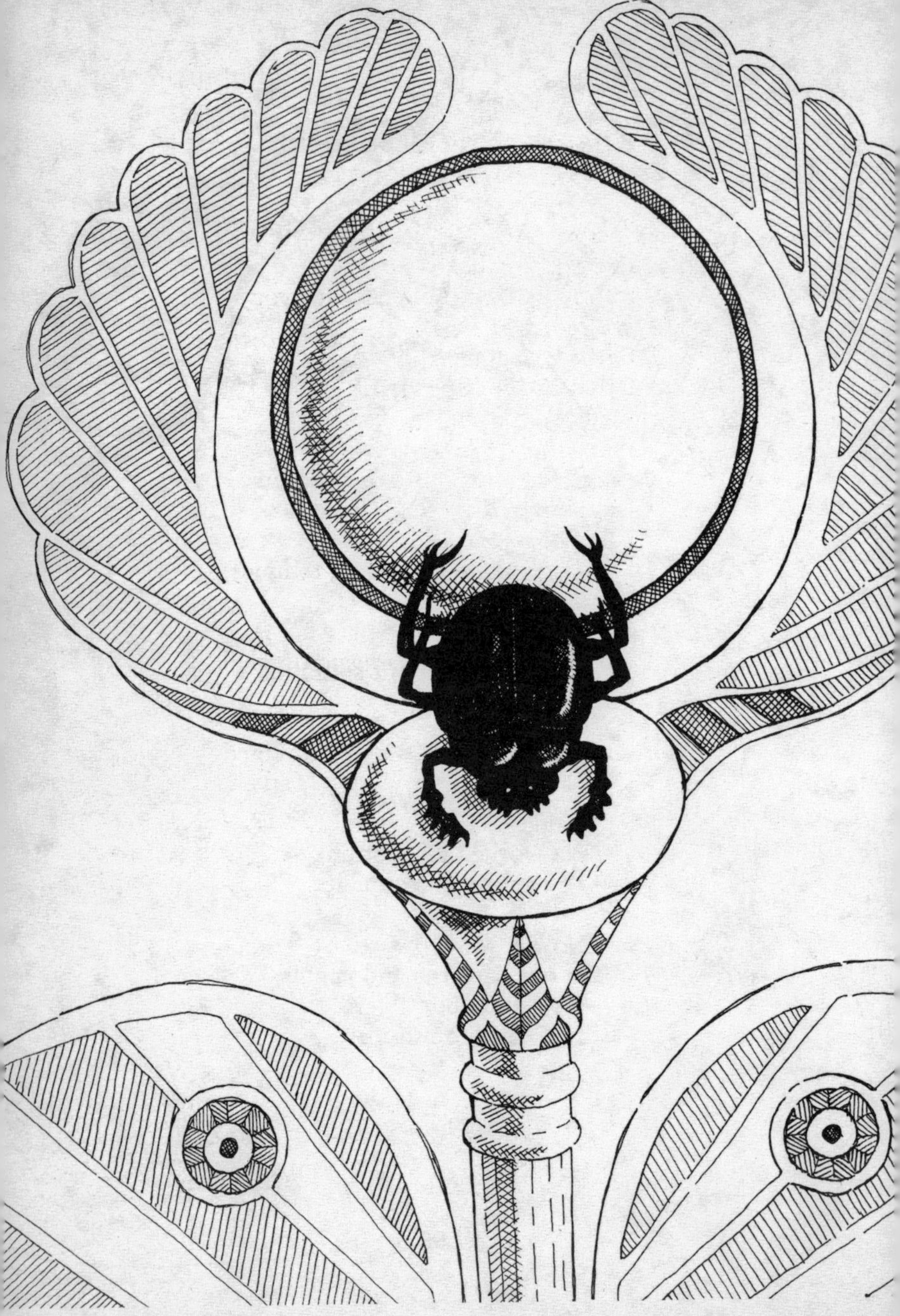

Khepra (The Dung Beetle)

See me now
low and small
rolling balls of dung beneath you,
See me then
Great God Ra
father of the King Osiris,
Made the days
with my labour
rolled the sun across the heavens,
I was high
I was holy
I had priests and towering temples,
But I made
too many journeys
and the mighty buildings crumbled,
See me then
see me now
Great God Khepra, lowly, humbled.

ROWENA SOMMERVILLE

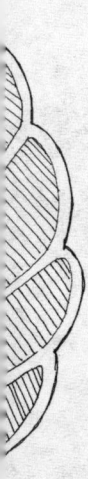

The Stick Insect

The stick insect
Isn't a very thick insect.
It's very hard to spot it.
If you want perfect camouflage
It's got it.

GAVIN EWART

Leapers and Creepers

The Lambton Worm

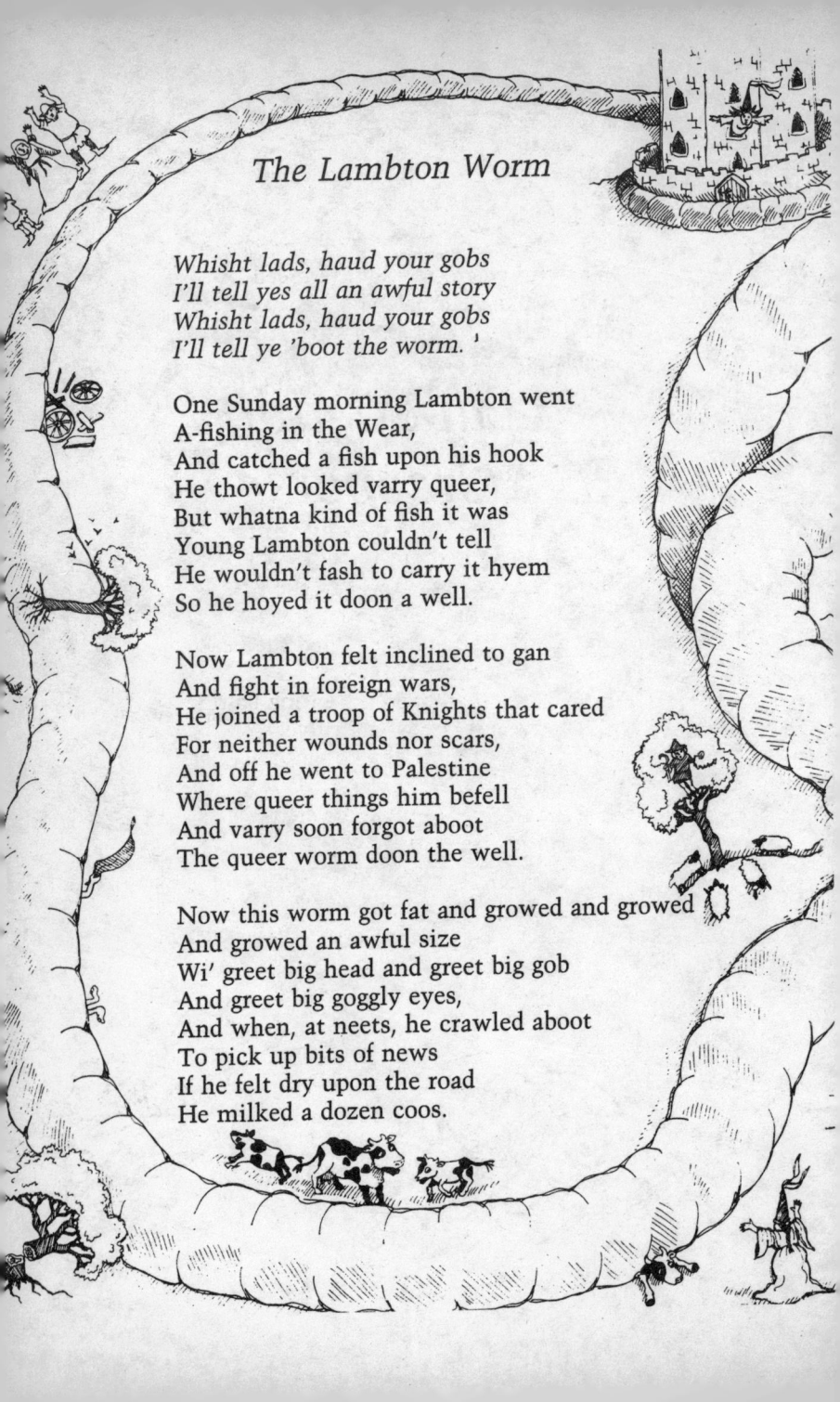

Whisht lads, haud your gobs
I'll tell yes all an awful story
Whisht lads, haud your gobs
I'll tell ye 'boot the worm.

One Sunday morning Lambton went
A-fishing in the Wear,
And catched a fish upon his hook
He thowt looked varry queer,
But whatna kind of fish it was
Young Lambton couldn't tell
He wouldn't fash to carry it hyem
So he hoyed it doon a well.

Now Lambton felt inclined to gan
And fight in foreign wars,
He joined a troop of Knights that cared
For neither wounds nor scars,
And off he went to Palestine
Where queer things him befell
And varry soon forgot aboot
The queer worm doon the well.

Now this worm got fat and growed and growed
And growed an awful size
Wi' greet big head and greet big gob
And greet big goggly eyes,
And when, at neets, he crawled aboot
To pick up bits of news
If he felt dry upon the road
He milked a dozen coos.

This awful worm would often feed
On calves and lambs and sheep
And swellied little bairns alive
When they lay doon to sleep.
And when he'd eaten all he could
And he had had his fill,
He crawled away and lapped his tail
Ten times round Penshaw Hill.

Now news of this most awful worm
And his queer gannins-on
Soon crossed the seas, got to the ears
Of brave and bold Sir John.
So hyem he come and catched the beast
And cut it in three halves.
And that soon stopped his eating bairns
And sheep and lambs and calves.

Now lads I'll haud me gob
That's all I know aboot the story
of Sir John's clever job
Wi' the famous Lambton Worm.

TRADITIONAL STORY

Snails

Sound of snails – crying,
Sound drifting through the brush, sound of crying.
Slime of snails, dragging themselves
Along the low-lying plain, crying;
Snails with their slime, crying.
Sound drifting through the bush:
Dragging themselves along, crying,
Snails, their sound blowing overhead from among the bushes.

LIAGARANG

The Sick Rose

O Rose, thou art sick.
The invisible worm,
that flies in the night
In the howling storm,

Has found out thy bed
of crimson joy;
And his dark secret love
Does thy life destroy.

WILLIAM BLAKE

The Tickle Rhyme

'Who's that tickling my back?' said the wall.
'Me,' said a small
Caterpillar. 'I'm learning
To crawl.'

IAN SERRAILLIER

Dissertation on the Antiquity of Fleas

'Adam
Had 'em'

ANON

Crunch Thwock

When I'm walking out at night,
Without a guiding light,
How I dread the tiny wails
Of a hundred scrambled snails.

They gather at my feet,
As for some snaily treat,
And lie in wait for me,
With suicidal glee,

And as I hold my breath,
They hurl themselves to death,
Like lemmings over cliffs,
From soggy-bods to stiffs.

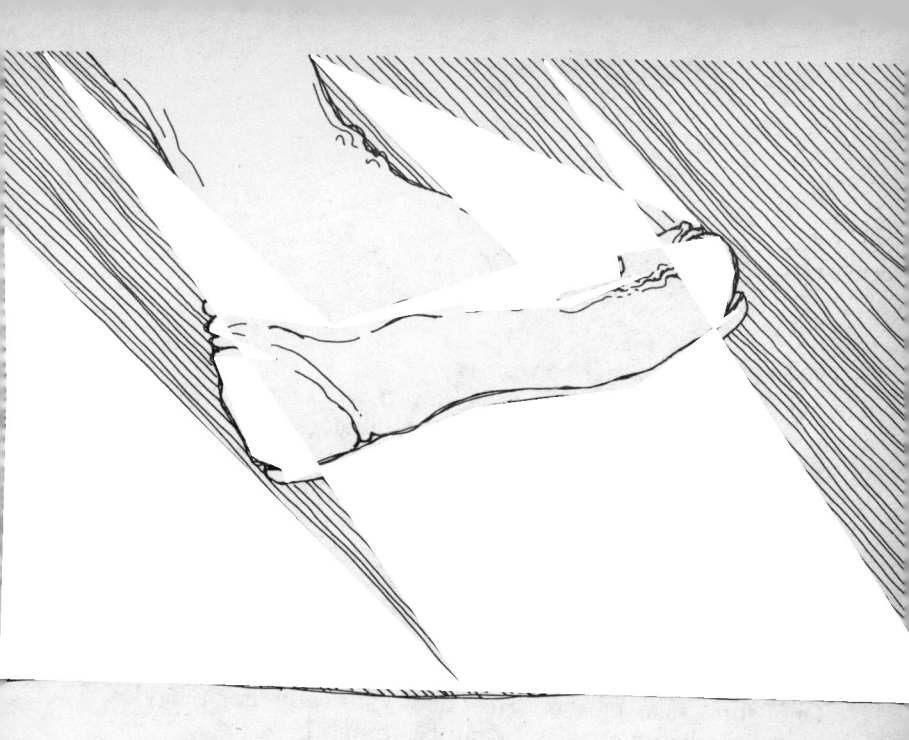

I hear that ghastly crack,
It's too late to step back,
And vital mollusc ooze
Is sticking to my shoes.

I'm overcome with guilt
As snail life-juice is spilt
And bubbles from grey pores –
I must retreat indoors.

In the morning what remains
Is a trail of crackly stains
That leads up to my porch –
I'll have to buy a torch!

ROWENA SOMMERVILLE

Worms and the Wind

Worms would rather be worms.
Ask a worm and he says, 'Who knows what a worm knows?'
Worms go down and up and over and under.
Worms like tunnels.
When worms talk they talk about the worm world.
Worms like it in the dark.
Neither the sun nor the moon interest a-worm.
Zigzag worms hate circle worms.
Curve worms never trust square worms.
Worms know what worms want.
Slide worms are suspicious of crawl worms.
One worm asks another, 'How does your belly drag today?'
A straight worm says, 'Why not be straight?'
Worms tired of crawling begin to slither.
Long worms slither farther than short worms.
Middle-sized worms say, 'It is nice to be
　neither long nor short.'
Old worms teach young worms to say,
'Don't be sorry for me unless you have been a worm and
　lived in worm places and read worm books.'
When worms go to war they dig in, come
　out again and fight, dig in
again, come out and fight again, dig in again and so on.
Worms underground never hear the wind
　overground and sometimes they ask,
'What is this wind we hear of?'

CARL SANDEURG

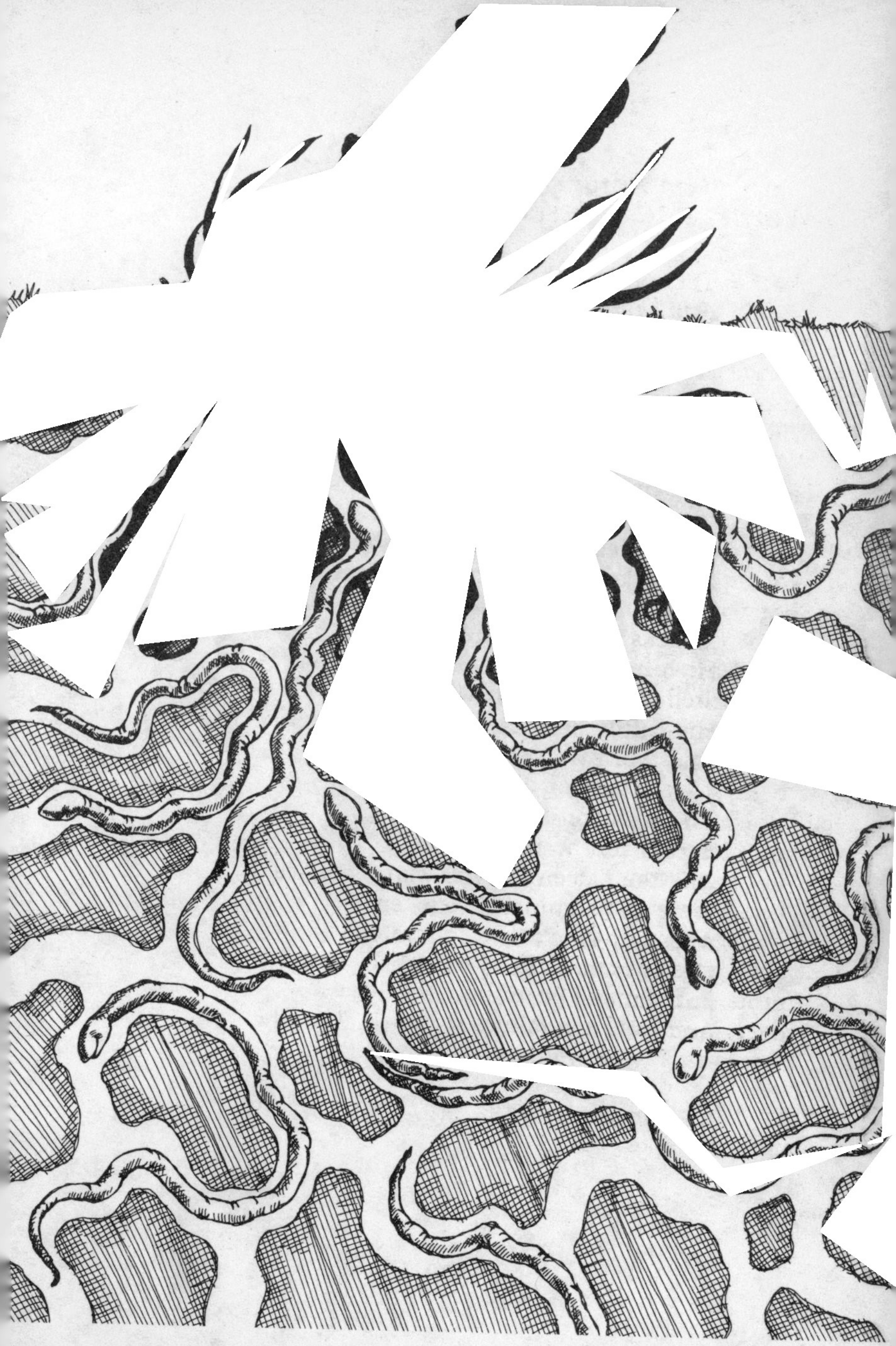

The Song of the Flea

There ruled a king long, long ago,
And he had a very fine flea,
Who could have been the King's own son,
He so adored that flea.
He called for his private tailor,
And when his tailor came
Cried, 'Measure my boy for breeches
And coats to go with the same!'

So the flea was dressed in velvets
And silks which were of the best,
He had ribbons on his clothing,
A cross was hung on his chest.
He became a minister soon,
So he wore a star as well,
His family became very grand at court,
And that gave the courtiers hell.

Those persons of both sexes
Excessively were bitten,
And the Queen and her waiting ladies
Were all abominably stricken,
And they didn't dare to scratch
Or catch those fleas and whack 'em –
But you and I can scratch
And we catch our fleas and crack 'em!

JOHANN VON GOETHE

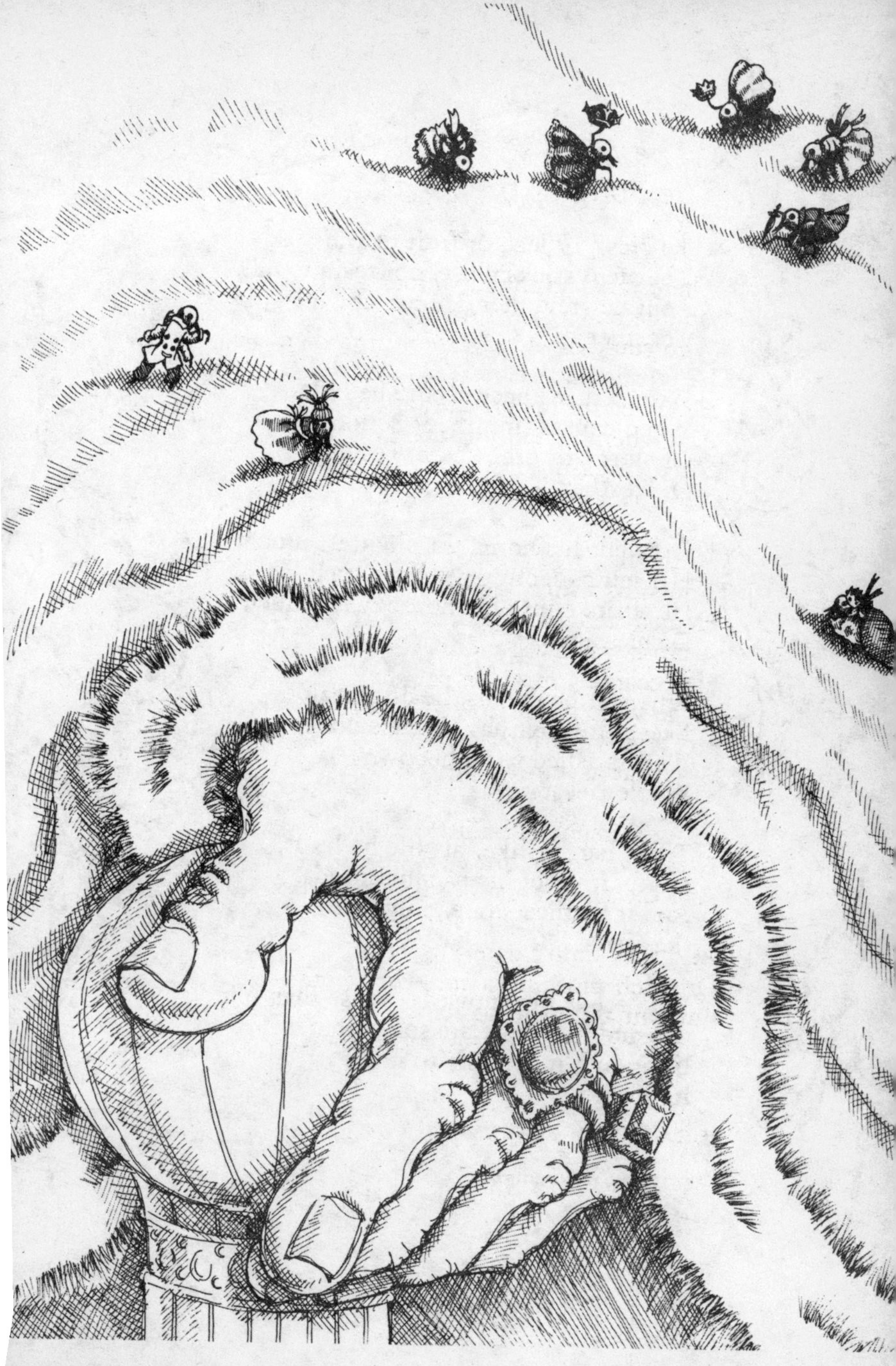

The Snail

To grass, or leaf, or fruit or wall,
The snail sticks close, nor fears to fall,
As if he grew there, house and all
Together.

Within that house secure he hides,
When danger imminent betides
Of storm, or other harm besides
Of weather.

Give but his horns the slightest touch,
His self-collecting power is such,
He shrinks into his house, with much
Displeasure.

Where'er he dwells, he dwells alone,
Except himself has chattels none,
Well satisfied to be his own
Whole treasure.

Thus, hermit-like, his life he leads,
Nor partner of his banquet needs,
And if he meets one, only feeds
the faster.

Who seeks him must be worse than blind,
(He and his home are so combin'd),
If, finding it, he fails to mind
Its master.

WILLIAM COWPER

Today I Saw A Little Worm

Today I saw a little worm
Wriggling on his belly.
Perhaps he'd like to come inside
And see what's on the telly.

SPIKE MILLIGAN

Surprise!

A worm once bit me on the knee,
The pain was agonising –
But since that worm was six foot three,
It isn't so surprising!

HELEN RATCLIFFE

Acknowledgements

The editors and publishers wish to thank the following for giving permission to include in this anthology material which is their copyright. If we have inadvertently omitted to acknowledge anyone we should be most grateful if this could be brought to our attention for correction at the first opportunity.

Moira Andrew for 'Nature Study' by Moira Andrew from *Another Fourth Poetry Book*, compiled by John Foster, published by Oxford University Press, 1989. Copyright © Moira Andrew 1989.

Curtis Brown Ltd, for 'The Termite' by Ogden Nash.

Gina Douthwaite for 'Spider' from *The Usborne Book of Animal Poems*.

Faber and Faber Limited for 'Bee' by George Barker from *The Alphabetical Animal Zoo*.

Eric Finney for 'Earwig O!' by Eric Finney, first published in *Another Third Poetry Book*, compiled by John Foster, published by Oxford University Press, 1988.

Pamela Gillilan for 'Mottled Moths' by Pamela Gillilan from *A Fifth Poetry Book*, published by Oxford University Press.

Harcourt Brace Jovanovich, Inc for 'Worms and the Wind' by Carl Sandburg from *The People Say Yes* and 'Adventure' by Louis Untermeyer, reprinted from 'Jade Butterflies' in *Roast Leviathan*.

William Heinemann Limited for 'Gone Locusts' by George Awoonor-Williams from *Young Commonwealth Poets*, edited by P L Brent.

Macmillan Publishers Ltd for 'The Butterfly and the Kite' by Raymond Wilson, adapted from Krylov, 'The Centipede' by Carmen Bernos de Gasztold, translated by Rumer Godden, and 'Spider' by Alan Brownjohn. Reprinted by permission of Macmillan Publishers Ltd.

Spike Milligan Productions Ltd, for 'Today I Saw a Little Worm' by Spike Milligan, from *Silly Verse for Kids*, published by Puffin Books.

Penguin Books Ltd for 'Cobweb Morning' from *The Jungle Sale* by June Crebbin, published by Viking Kestrel, 1988. Copyright © June Crebbin, 1988. Reproduced by permission of Penguin Books Ltd.

Random Century Group for 'The Stick Insect' by Gavin Ewart from *Caterpillar Stew*. Reprinted by permission of Hutchinson

Children's Books, an imprint of the Random Century Group.
Random House, Inc for 'Ants, Although Admirable, Are Awfully Aggravating' by Walter R Brooks from *The Collected Poems of Freddy the Pig*.
Helen Ratcliffe for 'Surprise', 'An Unconsidered Trifle' and 'A Gnat' by Helen Ratcliffe.
Scholastic Publications Ltd, for 'Look – Said the Boy' by Michael Rosen from *Wouldn't You Like to Know*.
Ian Serraillier for 'The Tickle Rhyme' by Ian Serraillier from *Catalogue of Comic Verse*, published by Hodder & Stoughton.
Transworld Publishers Ltd for 'A Game of Squash' by Dick King-Smith. Copyright © 1990 by Dick King-Smith. Extracted from *Jungle Jingles* published by Doubleday. All rights reserved. Reprinted by permission of Transworld Publishers Ltd.
Manley Young for 'Anancy the Spiderman' by Manley Young from *Mango Spice – Forty-four Caribbean Songs* (A & C Black).